SIMPLE MACHINE PROJECTS

Making Machines with Wheels and Axles

Chris Oxlade

heinemann raintree

Edited by James Benefield and Erika Shores
Designed by Steve Mead
Original illustrations © Capstone Global Library Ltd 2015
Picture research by Jo Miller
Production by Victoria Fitzgerald
Originated by Capstone Global Library Ltd
Printed and bound in China by Leo Paper Group

18 17 16 15 14
10 9 8 7 6 5 4 3 2 1

Library of Congress Cataloging-in-Publication Data
Oxlade, Chris, author.
  Making machines with wheels and axles / Chris Oxlade.
    pages cm.—(Simple machine projects)
  Includes bibliographical references and index.
  ISBN 978-1-4109-6804-3 (hb)—ISBN 978-1-4109-6811-1
(pb)—ISBN 978-1-4109-6825-8 (ebooks) 1. Wheels—Juvenile
literature. 2. Axles—Juvenile literature. 3. Simple machines—
Juvenile literature. I. Title.

  TJ181.5.O92 2015
  621.8'11—dc23   2014013824

**This book has been officially leveled by using the F&P Text
Level Gradient™ Leveling System.**

Acknowledgments
We would like to thank the following for permission to
reproduce photographs:

All photos Capstone Studio: Karon Dubke except: Dreamstime:
Benjamin Gelman, 15; Getty Images: Tim Graham, 9; Shut-
terstock: fimkaJane, 29 (top), Jo De Vulder, 20, mertcan, 6,
Monkey Business Images, 7, Pecold, 29 (bottom), Raimundas,
27, sydeen, 26, Tatiana Belova, 14, underworld, 4; UIG via
Getty Images: Universal History Archive, 8.

Design Elements: Shutterstock: Timo Kohlbacher.

We would like to thank Harold Pratt and Richard Taylor for
their invaluable help in the preparation of this book.

Every effort has been made to contact copyright holders
of material reproduced in this book. Any omissions will
be rectified in subsequent printings if notice is given to
the publisher.

All the Internet addresses (URLs) given in this book were valid
at the time of going to press. However, due to the dynamic
nature of the Internet, some addresses may have changed, or
sites may have changed or ceased to exist since publication.
While the author and publisher regret any inconvenience this
may cause readers, no responsibility for any such changes can
be accepted by either the author or the publisher.

CONTENTS

Some words are shown in bold, **like this**. You can find out what they mean by looking in the glossary.

WHAT ARE WHEELS AND AXLES?

When you ride your bike, steer a go-kart, or turn a faucet on or off, wheels and **axles** are helping you. A wheel and axle is a simple machine. In this book, you'll see many examples of wheels and axles, from the everyday to the extraordinary. The projects will help you to understand how wheels and axles work.

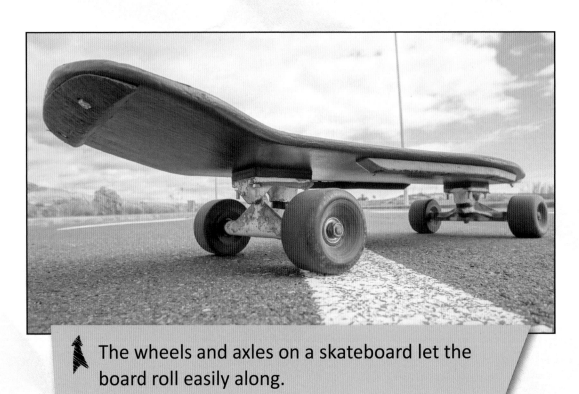

The wheels and axles on a skateboard let the board roll easily along.

SIMPLE MACHINES

Simple machines make our lives easier by helping us to move and lift heavy loads, fix things tightly in place, and cut tough materials. Wheels and axles are one of the five types of simple machines. The other four are the **pulley**, the **lever**, the **ramp** or the **wedge**, and the **screw**.

Wheels and axles around us

There are probably more wheels and axles around you than you think. Even a simple doorknob that you turn to open a door works with a wheel and axle. The diagram below explains a little more about these simple machines.

A wheel and axle is made up of a wheel joined to an axle (a rod).

wheel

axle

HOW WHEELS AND AXLES WORK

Wheels and axles help us in two different ways. Here we look at how they help us to move things along. They also make forces larger (see the box opposite) and change **motion** (see page 14).

Imagine pushing a heavy box along the ground, and then imagine pushing the box along on a skateboard. It's much easier to push it along on a skateboard. That's because wheels reduce **friction**. Friction is a force. It tries to stop surfaces from sliding past one other. Friction makes it hard to push a heavy box along the ground. Rolling wheels make much less friction, so a box on wheels is easier to move.

A box trolley has wheels and axles that make it easy to move heavy boxes from one place to another.

FORCE AND MOTION

Simple machines such as wheels and axles can change force and motion. A simple machine can make a force (a push or a pull) larger or smaller, or change its direction. It can also make a movement (motion) larger or smaller, or change its direction.

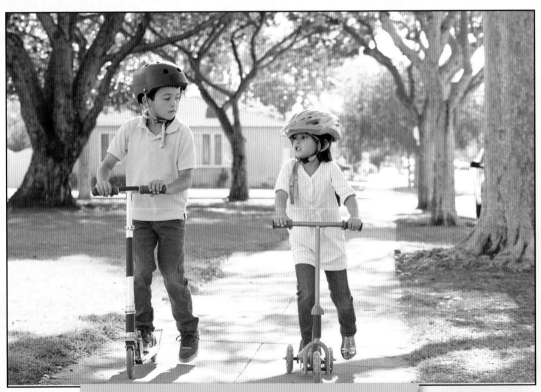

The wheels make it easy for these children to roll along.

WHEELS AND AXLES IN HISTORY

For many thousands of years, people moved objects by carrying them, by dragging them, or by getting an animal to carry them. Things got a lot easier when the wheel was invented. We don't know who invented the wheel, or exactly when or where—but it was probably around 5,500 years ago in the Middle East. The first wheels were used on simple carts.

This picture, carved over 2,500 years ago, shows spoked wheels on a hunting chariot.

Wheels for pottery

As people started putting wheels on carts, potters realized they could make pots with a wheel. To do this, potters place a wheel on its side. They put a blob of clay on the wheel and then turn the wheel. As the wheel turns, the potter presses on the clay to shape it into a neat circular pot.

WATER WHEELS

A water wheel is a large wheel with buckets around the rim. When water is poured into the buckets, the wheel turns. In the past, water wheels worked the **grindstones** in mills.

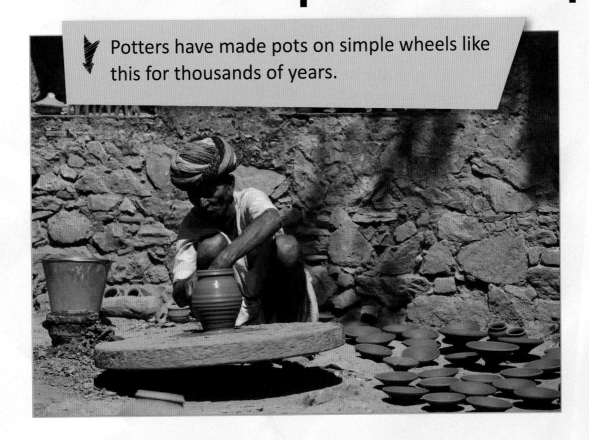

Potters have made pots on simple wheels like this for thousands of years.

Moving on Wheels

In this project, you'll be able to see what the effect of adding wheels to something is.

What you need:
- a small cardboard box, about 8 inches (20 cm) long and about 4 in. (10 cm) across
- some yarn
- a small plastic cup
- some marbles
- two long, sharp pencils
- some thick cardboard
- sticky tape
- scissors

1 Cut a piece of yarn 4 inches (10 cm) long. Attach one end of the piece of yarn to the end of the box. Put the box on your work surface, 1 in. (3 cm) or so back from the edge (see picture below).

STEP 1

2 Hang the yarn over the edge of the work surface. Tape the yarn into the inside of the cup.

3 Put marbles into the cup one by one, until the box slides across the table (see picture below). Write down how many marbles you needed.

STEP 3

4 Using a sharp pencil, make two holes in each side of the box. Make the holes half an inch up from the bottom and half an inch in from the box's ends.

5 Wiggle the pencil around in the holes so that the pencils can spin easily (see picture, right).

STEP 5

6 Draw four circles about 3 in. (8 cm) across on thick cardboard (you can use a can to draw around, if it's easier).

7 Cut out the circles carefully. Pierce a hole in the center of each circle.

STEP 7

8 Put a pencil through the holes you pierced at each end of the box. Push the wheels onto the ends of the pencils.

9 The vehicle is complete. Place it 2 in. (5 cm) from the edge of the work surface, and hang the yarn and cup over the edge.

10 Put marbles into the cup again one by one until the box moves.

STEP 10

What did you find out?

Friction stopped the box from moving easily before you added the wheels. It took fewer marbles to make the box move after you added the wheels. This shows that the wheels reduced friction.

CHANGING FORCE AND MOTION

A wheel and axle can change the degree of force. This is because the **diameter** of the wheel is greater than the diameter of the axle. Think about the steering wheel on a go-kart. The steering wheel is on the end of a rod, which is its axle. Small up-and-down pushes and pulls on the steering wheel make much larger pushes and pulls on the axle. This makes it easy to steer the go-kart.

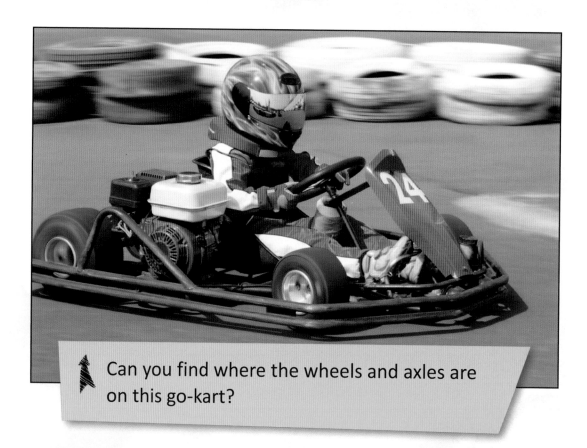

Can you find where the wheels and axles are on this go-kart?

Axles for spinning

Simple machines can also change motion. A simple spinning top (in the photo, below) is a wheel and axle. The triangle-like bottom part is the wheel, and the top part, the spindle, is the axle. A small movement of your fingers makes it move quickly. This is because the wheel and axle increases the speed of movement.

This spinning top is made up of a wheel at the bottom and an axle at the top.

spindle

BALANCING WHEELS

A gyroscope (say "jie-ruh-scope") is a balancing device with a heavy wheel that spins to keep it steady. Pulling a string that's wrapped around the wheel's axle makes the wheel turn at very high speed.

Lifting with a Wheel and Axle

This simple project will help you to understand how a wheel and axle can make a force larger.

What you need:
- some thin cardboard
- scissors
- sticky tape
- a long pencil
- yarn
- three identical washers

1 Cut a piece of cardboard 10 inches (25 cm) long and 2 in. (5 cm) wide.

2 Tape one end of the cardboard to the pencil, as shown below.

STEP 2

3 Wrap the cardboard tightly around the pencil (see picture, below). Tape down the end of the cardboard to stop the cardboard from unwrapping.

STEP 3

4 Cut another piece of cardboard 10 inches long and 2 inches wide. Stick it onto the wound-up cardboard and wrap it around as before. Cut and stick on a third piece of cardboard in the same way. The pieces of cardboard stuck around the pencil form a **drum**.

STEP 4

5 Cut two pieces of yarn, one about 3 foot (1 meter) long and one about 20 in. (50 cm) long.

6 Tape the end of the longer piece of yarn to the center of the drum (see picture below).

STEP 6

7 Tape a washer to the end of this piece of yarn. Spin the pencil slowly to wind the yarn onto the drum.

STEP 7

8 Now take the short piece of yarn and tape it to the pointed end of the pencil, as in the picture for step 9.

9 Tape two washers to the end of the shorter piece of yarn. Spin the pencil slowly to wind the yarn. Spin it in the opposite direction than you chose in step 7.

STEP 9

10 Hold the ends of the pencil like the picture and hold it at chest height. Release your grip to allow the pencil to spin.

STEP 10

What did you find out?
The drum and pencil worked like a wheel and axle. The smaller weight on the piece of yarn around the drum (the wheel) lifted the larger weight on the yarn around the pencil (the axle).

GEAR WHEELS

A **gear wheel** is a wheel with teeth around the rim (see the picture below).

Gear wheels are always used with other gear wheels. When the teeth of two gear wheels interlock, the wheels can turn one another. We use gear wheels to transfer movement from one axle to another. So, when you turn one axle, the other axle turns, too.

These toy gear wheels show how the teeth on gear wheels interlock with each other.

Changing speeds

We often use different sizes of gear wheels together. When you turn one wheel, the other wheel turns faster or slower than the first wheel. If the second wheel is larger, it turns more slowly. If the second wheel is smaller, it turns more quickly.

gear with 30 teeth

gear with 10 teeth

With these gear wheels, one turn of the large wheel turns the small wheel three times.

NANO GEARS

The word *nano* means "extremely small." Engineers have built experimental nano gear wheels that are too small to see with your eyes! They might be used in the future in tiny machines.

Making Gear Wheels

In this project, you will make two model gear wheels and see how they turn one another.

What you need:
- a CD or DVD (make sure it's an old one that you are allowed to use)
- a tin can
- two sharp pencils
- strong scissors
- some thick cardboard
- 10 popsicle sticks
- all-purpose glue

1 Draw around a CD on thick cardboard. Cut out the circle.

2 Draw around a can that's about 3 inches (8 cm) across. Cut out the circle (see below for what the circles will look like).

STEP 2

3 On the large circle, draw lines at the positions of the 12 numbers on a clock face (ask an adult to help).

4 On the small circle, draw eight lines, equally spaced around the circle (see picture, right).

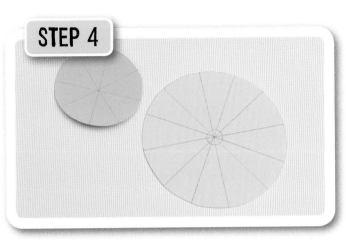

STEP 4

5 Draw a line 1 in. (3 cm) from the end of each popsicle stick. Ask an adult to cut across the sticks at the lines with strong scissors (see picture below).

STEP 5

6 Glue a popsicle stick end to one of the circles at the end of one of the lines, as shown below.

7 Now glue a popsicle stick end on all the other lines. Turn the circles over and let the glue dry.

STEP 6

8 Cut a piece of cardboard about 10 x 6 in. (25 x 15 cm). Mark the halfway point up each of the shorter sides of the cardboard and draw a line to join these. Along this center line, make two marks on the cardboard, 4½ in. (11½ cm) across.

STEP 9

9 With a sharp pencil, pierce holes in the cardboard at the two marks. Wiggle the pencil until it can spin freely.

10 Push a pencil through the circles' centers.

11 Put the pencils through the holes in cardboard sheet so that the gear wheels line up.

12 Turn the small wheel. The large wheel will turn, too.

STEP 12

What did you find out?

You will see that the gear wheels turn in opposite directions. The wheels have a different number of teeth. It takes three turns of the small wheel to make the large wheel turn twice.

WHEELS AND AXLES IN COMPLEX MACHINES

Many complex machines are made up of simple machines such as wheels and axles.

Of course, complex machines such as trucks and trains need wheels and axles to move along roads or railroad tracks. But they also have wheels and axles inside them. Engines and gearboxes are full of wheels, axles, and gear wheels. These make forces larger and smaller, or make moving parts go faster or slower.

Gearboxes contain wheels and axles of different sizes.

Shaped wheels

Some machines contain wheels that are shaped to produce movement. These special wheels are called cams. As a cam turns, it pushes a lever up or lets it fall. You can see cams at work in some wooden toys.

CLOCK AND WATCH GEARS

Clocks and watches contain gears that control the speeds of the hands. A motor turns the second hand. Gears slow this movement down to move the minute hand and hour hand at the correct speeds.

 The inside of a clock contains wheels shaped to produce movement.

FACTS AND FUN

AMAZING WHEELS AND AXLES

The wheels on the world's largest dump truck (the 546-ton Belaz 75710) are a monster 13 feet (4 meters) tall. The truck has eight wheels in total.

The world's largest working water wheel is the Laxey Wheel on the Isle of Man. It's an amazing 72 feet (22 meters) across. That's the same as the height of a seven-story building.

The engineers will soon complete the world's largest Ferris wheel, the Dubai Wheel. It will be 689 feet (210 meters) across.

Scientists in Singapore have built a tiny, tiny gear wheel just 1.2 nanometers across. If 1 million of these gear wheels were lined up side by side, the line would be just over a millimeter long.

WHEELS AND AXLES TODAY

All simple machines, including wheels, were invented thousands of years ago. Wheels and axles are even more important today than they were in the past—we travel so much today. And wheels and axles will certainly be useful for many years to come!

What and where are the wheels and axles?

Can you see a wheel and axle in action here?

What is making the wheel turn in this photo?

GLOSSARY

axle rod that is attached to the center of a wheel

diameter distance from one side of a circle to the other, which is measured from the center

drum cylinder that a rope or string is wound around

friction force that tries to stop two touching surfaces (such as the floor and the sole of a shoe) from sliding past each other

gear wheel wheel that has teeth around its rim that interlock with the teeth on another gear wheel

grindstones two stones, one on top of the other, that grind wheat between them when the top wheel turns

lever long bar that is pushed or pulled against a fulcrum to help move heavy loads or cut material

motion movement

pulley simple machine made up of wheels and rope, used to lift or pull objects

ramp simple machine used to lift heavy objects

screw simple machine that has a spiral-shaped thread, used to attach or lift materials

wedge simple machine used to split apart materials

FIND OUT MORE

Books

Deane-Pratt, Ade. *Simple Machines* (How Things Work).
   New York: PowerKids, 2012.

Gosman, Gillian. *Wheels and Axles in Action* (Simple Machines
   at Work). New York: PowerKids, 2011.

Walker, Sally M., and Roseann Feldmann. *Put Wheels and
   Axles to the Test* (How Do Simple Machines Work? Minn.:
   Lerner, 2012.

Web sites

Facthound offers a safe, fun way to find
Internet sites related to this book. All
of the sites on Facthound have been
researched by our staff.

Here's all you do:
Visit *www.facthound.com*
Type in this code: 9781410968043

INDEX